The Greatest Love Story Never T(
Sample

The Greatest Love Story Never Told

A Collection of Poetry

by Rebecca Routh-Sample

The Greatest Love Story Never Told by Rebecca Routh-Sample

All rights reserved. This book or any portion thereof may not be produced in any manner without the express written permission of the author. Brief quotations are okay in review.

ISBN 978-1-4457-9573-7

Copyright 2024 by Rebecca Routh-Sample

Published 2024 by Lulu Press Inc

The Greatest Love Story Never Told by Rebecca Routh-Sample

9 781445 795737

The Greatest Love Story Never Told by Rebecca Routh-Sample

Other books by Rebecca Routh-Sample

Fiction

Diary Of A Teenage Fangirl

Diary Of A Teenage Rebel Girl

Poetry

ghost world

donnie darko

paramour

Spinner's End

The Greatest Love Story Never Told

Maybe You Never Loved Me As Much As You Loved New York

If You're Reading This, I Have Some Questions

The Greatest Love Story Never Told by Rebecca Routh-Sample

All available to purchase on www.lulu.com and www.Amazon.com

The Greatest Love Story Never Told by Rebecca Routh-Sample

Connect with me on social media if you want! I'd love to hear your feedback:

Twitter: @itsbeccafy

Instagram: @beccafyofficial

TikTok: @itsbeccafy

The Greatest Love Story Never Told by Rebecca Routh-Sample

Contents

1. I'm The Main Character
2. The Traitor
3. Instant
4. Valentine's Day
5. Electricity
6. Time With You
7. Talk To Me
8. Sweet Baby Angel
9. Fireworks
10. Pygmalion
11. Sleeper Cell
12. Nothing Used To Love You
13. Substance
14. Loyalty Card
15. A Different You
16. Elastoplast
17. Game Boy
18. Evangelion
19. Call Me Up
20. Pendulum
21. Trust Fund, Baby

The Greatest Love Story Never Told by Rebecca Routh-Sample

22. The Greatest Love Story Never Told
23. I Don't Have To Drown Again
24. Ballad To My Lover
25. Dreams
26. Gone
27. I Feel Like A Kid Again

The Greatest Love Story Never Told by Rebecca Routh-Sample

I'm The Main Character

I broke free from your chains
running faster than the speed
of light I adored you would've
stayed in one place all my life
stagnant, never moving never
growing never left broke out of
the prison of your love you
destroy every person you love
you're so busy running you
can't see who's behind you
took an arrow to the chest there
are no perks to being lied

to

I couldn't breathe I would just seethe
you spoke in tongues like some kind
of high priest beware, beware you're
coming round the corner don't let

The Greatest Love Story Never Told by Rebecca Routh-Sample

'em catch you but they're gonna
catch you

No prison break No
sympathy yesterday's news
like a bad movie No tears
no justice just sweet,
sweet, revenge I'd save
you some grace but I have
none left I learned to love
myself just as much as i
loved you if someone
wants to enter my life they
can come through but i'll
always hold me down just
like I held you
I'm the main character
you're just pretending

The Greatest Love Story Never Told by Rebecca Routh-Sample

The Traitor

All I ever wanted to do Was defend

And protect you

But you switched up

And made me look like a fool Yes, and

I must admit

Maybe I spoke too soon

So call me in nine months

When you've finally exited the womb

The only reason somebody could

act so brand new

I'll sip my sweet tea

While you pour salt in

your wounds I'll run

away

With my silver

The Greatest Love Story Never Told by Rebecca Routh- Sample

And quickly

Forget you

You could've had it all

You idiot

You tool

You could've had it all

Now you're a criminal

Back up against the wall

You could've had it all

When no one was on your side

I defended you

When no one believed your lies

At least I pretended to

I was in the getaway car

When she rear-ended you

I must have been so high

The Greatest Love Story Never Told by Rebecca Routh-Sample

To fall for you

I'll never make the same mistake again

I'll never take lies of a villain

For the words of a friend

Instant

Instant

Instant gratification

Instant likes

Perpetual entertainment

Perpetual vice

Self indulgence

The Greatest Love Story Never Told by Rebecca Routh- Sample

Self absorbed

Take in the vile Vomit on

the floor What you

input

Is what comes out

Rot your brain

Rot your mouth

But fill your life with love and joy

Something only the righteous will enjoy I try but I'm

addicted Post another picture

Ignore another pic

Madness on a screen

I'm obsessed

Instant queen   Instant

likes

Instant fans

Instant pleasure in my hands

The Greatest Love Story Never Told by Rebecca Routh-Sample

I can't cope with the world outside

I'll just take my screen and hide

Electricity

Electricity   met them in a bar, birthday
month thought they were real but i only
had a hunch and to be held

by the gentlest strongest force that has ever been was
electricity to me and the conductor conducted the
strings in my heart as my mouth was trying to tear my
words apart and they came out all crumbled and
matted and I wanted to to shout:

I don't want to leave this place

I don't even wanna live if I can't ever see your face and

I don't know how and I don't know why you're electricity

to me but it came out as a cry   Valentine's Day

The Greatest Love Story Never Told by Rebecca Routh-Sample

Glass hurting

Just like knives

Scars all over your thighs

Old Valentine's Day cards

Filled with lies

Advent calendar

The 25 days you tried

To leave

Over, and over again

You watched the news

You try to forget but then

A trigger, a whisper, a word Brings

back the trauma Brings back the

hurt You try to run away from

it

But it catches up to you

The Greatest Love Story Never Told by Rebecca Routh-Sample

Like a spider's web in the corner

of the room The pain it grows

Like a baby in the room Trauma has

a way

of catching up to you

Time With You

Picking petals off of the flowers you gave

me

Call me only by the name that you gave me Nobody ever has to know

But I want everyone to know

Because they think they know

But they don't

And I know my funny valentine knows

I need to let go

The Greatest Love Story Never Told by Rebecca Routh-Sample

I want my time with you

St. Pancras station

Where I wait for you I

never liked the South

but I'll go there for you

I just want my time with

you

I want my time with you

Burning hell   Where I wait

for you I always preferred

heaven but I'll leave there

for you I just want my

time with you

Talk To Me

I'm still stuck in that same old place

The Greatest Love Story Never Told by Rebecca Routh-Sample

Feather weather friends and fits of rage

Primordial soup and twisted games

'Let me in!'

You say

I drive all night

Just to reach the next day

Take a pill

Why don't you swallow?

Scared of it?

Why don't you let it follow?

If it's just a movie?

Why are you screaming

If it was a stupid mistake Why are you leaving?

Okay,

The Greatest Love Story Never Told by Rebecca Routh-Sample

Now it really is a horror story

Drive all night

Until it's morning

Heavy breathing

Twist around the room

Spider spider spider

Laying eggs in a barren room

I drove all night

Just to reach the next day

Sweet Baby Angel

I know it's been a long time

Normally you can't leave heaven And fall in love with our kind

And then when you did

The Greatest Love Story Never Told by Rebecca Routh-Sample

You fell in a love a demon

Her true intentions were hid

She was a soul-sucking heathen

All you talent, all your coins

All your adoration, all your joy

And you had to play the part

That tag-along boy toy

When you're the star of the screen

You fell down from heaven just for me

The first was a demon, the second my good friend But third time's the charm Sweet Baby Angel What then?

The conductor of the orchestra

Works his musicians to the bone

Harder tasks to master

Vicious lines you just have to know

But if you play the same play

Every year

The Greatest Love Story Never Told by Rebecca Routh-Sample

You're never gonna grow

And if you don't leave

The theatre

Then you'll never know

The touch of a hand   The

sparks of a kiss

Love and happiness

Radiating from your fingertips

And a real home

Just for you and me

A place where you can be happy

Sweet baby

Fireworks

Fireworks

The Greatest Love Story Never Told by Rebecca Routh-Sample

Tired words

Fire birds

Rub it out

Break it down

Tired nerves I

was   once

Painless

Not in hurts

Taxi, busy streets

I concur Grey's

Anatomy I got a

better body on me

Rise like a Phoenix I

wave a white flag

like a dove

And the blackness Pinpricked with

little lights

aeroplanes satellites Ernest wishes

The Greatest Love Story Never Told by Rebecca Routh-Sample

Hopes of peace Sweet

nothings you wish you

heard

Fireworks

Pygmalion

You were a big man now you're a big girl's blouse You were a spaceman but now you won't leave your house I was your wife Now you're just playing house You're growing older and she's younger right now but who's gonna be there are the end of time? When the sea turns red and the moon's low in the sky?

When all life's follies have passed you by When you have no more tears left to cry?

The Greatest Love Story Never Told by Rebecca Routh-Sample

Because you've seen it all who do

you think you are? Playing God

trying to mould a new true love out

of stone? women are born, they

aren't grown And I am the real

one the real one Life always kicks

hope out of you in the end   Take

my hand, I'm not a fair weather

friend

It's raining again Give

you my umbrella,

we're back to us again.

Sleeper Cell

Pierce   those   piercing

The Greatest Love Story Never Told by Rebecca Routh-Sample

bloodshot eyes that glisten

in the dark back in 2012

when you had my school girl

heart and you were just an

actor A person on a screen

A million miles apart my first

love first broken heart slam

into the glass right in the

kitchen bloody heroin veins

made up

Polynesian names I'm

choking drowning in the

ocean sewing up my

wounds a stitch in time

saves nine

Who's your latest victim?

Who's has your latest curse?

Which one was she? the one

being buried in the Earth did she

The Greatest Love Story Never Told by Rebecca Routh-Sample

cackle like a witch? did she have

self respect like a bitch?

where's your master of spin's spinning wheel?

I touch it so see if its real

It wasn't   I got

tricked and

every since

then

I've never a good night's sleep there's a chain of

memories and you're sleeper cell and I really mean it

when i say

I don't wish you well

Nothing Used To Love You

Nothing used to love you

sometimes i feel like

nothing nothing good at

least sometimes I feel

The Greatest Love Story Never Told by Rebecca Routh- Sample

empty devoid of anything
or anything good at least
nothing used to love you
nothing was a movie star
nothing was everything
nothing was your heart
everyone knew nothing It
wasn't only you nothing
knew everything but never
told the truth I used to love
nothing but nothing never
loved me nothing used to
love you but nothing never
knew me

Substance

Everything lacks substance everyone
I know is morally repugnant

The Greatest Love Story Never Told by Rebecca Routh-Sample

emotionally redundant You do every single thing you know you shouldn't for being on so much substance you think you'd have more substance what every happened   to spilling your feelings in a jumper and a second hand guitar sing you the crowd like how you'd sing to an empty bar after the signing you live a quiet life   doesn't answer the phone no insecurity

Because you know you earned all your stripes the world doesn't revolve around you you're not the moon you're not the sun you're just a girl and you want to have fun

Loyalty Card

The Greatest Love Story Never Told by Rebecca Routh-Sample

Watching old interviews of you my own personal form of self-harm remembering the pitter patter of your beating heart it was there and then it wasn't you were my trigger and you pulled the gun

ran away with evidence in that old sport bag you burn it to bits but your girl lies about what's in it it wasn't socks and shit it was the remnants of a love that was actually real remember how that that used to feel? drowning in a soul not in mass appeal   I don't have the energy to care anymore

The Greatest Love Story Never Told by Rebecca Routh-Sample

I'm just tired but you know

that they know that you

know   how it transpired

what went down the man

I admired

I'm handing my loyalty card

I'm giving up on love because it's

a very expensive hit and run   A

Different You

I'm scared of what's coming but

it's necessary growing up is

kind of scary but I think it's

crucial heroes fall and people

leave lightning doesn't always

strike twice

you lose your best friend, you

lose the love of your life but

The Greatest Love Story Never Told by Rebecca Routh-Sample

the new times the bad times

the long nights the light that

shines

It's worth running towards

at the end there's a

different you say goodbye

to your past you can't

take it with you

Elastoplast

It frustrates me how magic always

comes with madness I really

thought smoke and mirrors   could

distract from my badness

I'm bad, but am I bad to the core?

do cut you up, devour you and

leave you on the kitchen floor? I

asked the people who really know

The Greatest Love Story Never Told by Rebecca Routh-Sample

me but there was nobody to ask

growing up I tried to make

fairweather friends out of

elastoplast band-aid the pain

waiting for the last train

Game Boy

Living in dreams because it keeps

me from dying

I keep   an album in my phone full

of compliments don't want to be

seen outside in my hometown

but I'll spill

my guts to other continents I

really thought you'd stop

ghosting my heart but now

you're haunting it he's smoothing

me over   but i still think about all

The Greatest Love Story Never Told by Rebecca Routh-Sample

the lessons that you taunt me

since stop playing games boy

Peter Pan,

get off your game boy you

have no game boy

you can do better get away from

that man's wife if it's not for

fame boy why she play you like

a fool like tin boy you think

you're made of metal but your

skin isn't think boy inked all the

cuts and bruises lost ends tied

into nooses one more bad day

and you'll lose it when you're

warranty is out of date she'll go

find a new boy in another state

or a second marriage to that

lunatic that lives out of state

know a lot about her family

The Greatest Love Story Never Told by Rebecca Routh-Sample

don't know much about yours
know a lot about her kids What
about yours? your hopes and
dreams and when it's stops
being free and easy when the
money runs out court
appearances and the day they
try to take your life away

Evangelion

Don't let me get in the eva

If the vibes ain't right

If you aren't ready to

Rip the angels limb from limb I'm not gonna fight

I'm gonna crawl back into the womb and
then it's on sight If you got me and
we're winning we'll survive the night not

The Greatest Love Story Never Told by Rebecca Routh-Sample

the first impact to hit Tokyo I love you, I

love you baby left an angel in the snow

come back soon

I miss you

It's too hot in california

They're all brain dead

Call me harry styles

'cause I adore you like it's

the only thing

I'll ever do

I keep coming back to you

Call Me Up

Called you up last

night just to check

that you're alright   I

could scream

The Greatest Love Story Never Told by Rebecca Routh-Sample

I could cry

I could take a life but you tell me to

calm down

and it'll all be fine

Late one night in the depths of winter

I called out of the blue right after

you'd already kissed her but I

needed to you to know if I really

loved you I had to let you go and I let

myself go too

I don't think it's right but I had to let

you live even though it isn't your

best life I need you to

know you'll be alright even if you relapse even if

you scream in the middle of the night take a blade

to your chest and try to end the night

The Greatest Love Story Never Told by Rebecca Routh-Sample

I'll be there in the morning

lay your head on my shoulder

no matter who falls for you

you'll always be mine Call me

up, anytime

Pendulum

I'm sick and tired of having to

pretend i'm dumb conversations

swinging back and forth like a

pendulum pretending I can't

remember where it's swung

back to me, back to you well

the time has come meet me in

the hallway

waiting, waiting, all day

The Greatest Love Story Never Told by Rebecca Routh-Sample

Trust Fund, Baby

Trust Fund Baby playing

it cool

you pushed me into the swimming pool

trust me baby, you're a fucking tool and

if you're nep didn't tism you'd have

dropped out of school but don't worry

your parents names are blue indie

musician with not much to do self

made billionaire out of work actor with

time to spare boarding school but

there on a scholarship family in the

monarchy but you claim you wanna

abolish it if your nep didn't tism

you'd be living on the streets 'I'm

not a Tory' you say in Waitrose

wearing second hand clothes you

The Greatest Love Story Never Told by Rebecca Routh-Sample

bought on Asos marketplace that

originally belonged to a heroin

user that overdosed I asked her

how to make it and she said

'trust fund, baby'

The Greatest Love Story Never Told

If I could take a life to

have you in mine I

would you know baby I

would you know your

new girl could help me

get away with it but i

don't think she would I

want to have kids with

you I want to build a

home with you you

deserve better than to

The Greatest Love Story Never Told by Rebecca Routh- Sample

copy and paste
yourself into someone
else's life be with
someone else's wife
you deserve a better
ending to the greatest
love story never told I
could write you a symphony I
could
write you a song I
could want in the rain
all night long but you
have your boundaries
and I'm
crazy as hell or maybe
you just got me under
your spell

I Don't Have To Drown Again

The Greatest Love Story Never Told by Rebecca Routh-Sample

They said

I'd never get far in life may as

well be a house wife take me with

a pinch of salt lynch ideas that

don't seem right but I have

personal autonomy bursting from

the seems I have the intention to

do however I please and I

thought pushing myself to the

point of destruction

would serve them right because achievement

means nothing

If you're unhappy in your personal life

I'm vulnerable and open but I don't

suffer fools I know how it feels to let your

wrists split open as I drown into the

bottom of a swimming pool but he

reaches out his hand like an old friend   I

The Greatest Love Story Never Told by Rebecca Routh-Sample

don't have to drown again you're my

dearest friend

I don't have to drown again

Ballad To My Lover

I wake up

It's just another day without

you soaked in rain burning

in pain twisted games slice

of cake game we played

plans we made like puzzle

pieces on the floor

sunglasses in the drawer

listening to one of the boys,

evermore touching lips

grazing hips forgotten

prince I'm remised

to say 'I love you'

The Greatest Love Story Never Told by Rebecca Routh-Sample

There is no one above you if

I could go back then

I'd tell myself you're my only friend

wandering in wanderlust nothing

compares to us hold me sweetly,

truly, madly, deeply drug-fueled,

manic, melancholy panic tantric,

sadist, like I am the baddest tell me

truly, madly you leave am I like the

ones before? those beautiful girls

with poor social mores but I love

you like a lunatic follow your sister

and her friends drink that turmeric

let's go down

the rabbit hole those lies, those lies,

you stole so pretty but all of a

sudden it hit me I bet you anything

we're gonna make them sing like

The Greatest Love Story Never Told by Rebecca Routh-Sample

the joy that brings like pretty little things lined

up in a row

Dreams

I had a dream last night a
boy I used to love pretended
he didn't know me my love
knew no bounds he didn't
want to know me my big
brother tell me you still care I
only see you a through a
screen but i'm always there
in reality there's a tear you're
the sweetest softest boy and
you need to get out of there
come back to me those
dreams that Los Angeles rips
at the seems

The Greatest Love Story Never Told by Rebecca Routh-Sample

Gone

Sometimes I wish

I didn't feel as much as I do sometimes

I wish

I never loved you how on
earth am I supposed go on
with life with your room next
to me?

I can't breathe

I can't breathe only cry I just miss
you say you'll be here soon I just
miss you let me miss you let me
kiss you one last time the best
person in my life I've to convey
this so many times   I didn't know

The Greatest Love Story Never Told by Rebecca Routh-Sample

love until you loved me and I

didn't know trust until

you trusted me why

can't I hold you one

last time? graves are

so deep days are so

long life is so short

when you're gone you're

gone   everything   is

permanent but nothing stay

the same for too

long

If I could bring you back   I'd always bring you back   I Feel Like A Kid Again

I feel like a kid again driving

home from school I wish I

was going to you my

mother and my father and

my

The Greatest Love Story Never Told by Rebecca Routh-Sample

grandmother   and
grandfather and aunt I wish
I was kid again before I let
anyone down I wish you
were mine

I wish we were fine

I miss it all

I just want to go back to you
cricket matches cousins
playing Rugby fireworks in the
sky cotton candy Scarborough
beach caravans and those
animal ornaments collecting
ladybirds coming home from
the playground slipping through
the back window Nintendo DS
my goth best friends manga
spin the bottle not doing well in
french the smell of my mam's

The Greatest Love Story Never Told by Rebecca Routh-Sample

hair

I wish I was still there

I wish I was still there

If I could go back in time

I'd go back all the time

The Greatest Love Story Never Told by Rebecca Routh-Sample

All rights reserved. This book or any portion thereof may not be produced in any manner without the express written permission of the author. Brief quotations are okay in review.

ISBN 978-1-4457-9573-7

Copyright 2024 by Rebecca Routh-Sample

Published 2024 by Lulu Press Inc

The Greatest Love Story Never Told by Rebecca Routh-Sample

9 781445 795737

L - #0058 - 210325 - C0 - 210/148/3 - PB - DID4476120